The publishers wish to acknowledge the kind assistance of
Dr Pat Morris and Mr Michael Chinery in the preparation of this book.

© 1976, 1982 by Grisewood & Dempsey Ltd

Designed and produced by Grisewood & Dempsey Ltd,
Elsley Court, 20-22 Great Titchfield Street, London W1

Published in 1982 in this edition by Galley Press,
an imprint of W H Smith and Son Limited
Registered No 237811 England.
Trading as WHS Distributors, St John's House,
East Street, Leicester, LE1 6NE

ISBN 0 86136 951 3

Printed and bound in Portugal by Printer Portuguesa, Sintra.

The Bumblebee

By Angela Sheehan
Illustrated by Maurice Pledger

Galley Press

Each day the spring sun became warmer. The birds woke earlier and earlier, and sang for joy that the winter had passed. The bumblebee queen had spent all the winter in a tiny hole under a stone. As the sun warmed the stone the queen bee woke. Still drowsy, she crawled from her comfortable hiding place. The cool air blowing against the hairs on her back made her cold, and she felt very weak. She had had no food for more than six months.

But the sun soon made her warmer, and she stretched her wings and flew to a pussy willow tree that stood nearby. Clusters of catkins covered in yellow pollen clothed its branches. The queen bee settled down to her first meal, of pollen and nectar.

For a few weeks, the queen bee did nothing but feed herself and bathe in the warm sunshine. At night she hid under stones or fallen leaves. But she needed a safer place to build a nest.

At the foot of the wall that ran by the side of the farm, there was a small hole. The hole had once been the home of a field mouse. But now the mouse had gone.

The queen bee found the hole and crawled in. Deep inside there was plenty of dry grass and leaves. It was a perfect place for the queen to lay the eggs that were growing inside her body.

Inside a space hardly bigger than an egg cup, the queen bee started to make a little wax cell, shaped like a cup. The wax came from the queen's body. She made it from the pollen she had eaten.

As soon as the cell was finished, the queen flew off to gather food from a clump of bluebells near the nest. Loaded with nectar and pollen, she returned and half-filled the cell. Then she pushed her tail into it and laid her eggs. There were ten in all. Over them, she placed a cap of wax so that the cell was completely sealed. Inside, the growing grubs would have plenty of food.

The queen, too, needed a store of food. So she made another little cell just inside the nest. Day by day, she collected more nectar and filled the 'honey-pot' with it. On rainy days, when she could not go out, the queen would still have plenty to eat.

For about five days, the only thing the queen could do for her young was to keep them as warm as possible. She clung to the outside of the wax cell and her furry body was like a thick blanket.

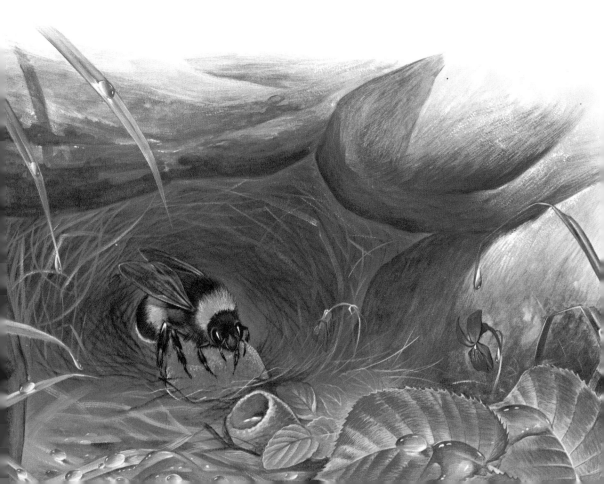

After five days, the eggs hatched into little
wriggling grubs. Soon they had finished all the food
in their cell. So the queen gnawed through the wax
cap and fed them through the hole. She also had to
make the cell larger to give them room to move.
On a rich diet of nectar and pollen, the grubs grew
bigger and bigger.

When the grubs were fully grown, each one
spun a thread of silk. Turning round and round and
round, they twisted the silk around their bodies to
make warm, soft cocoons.

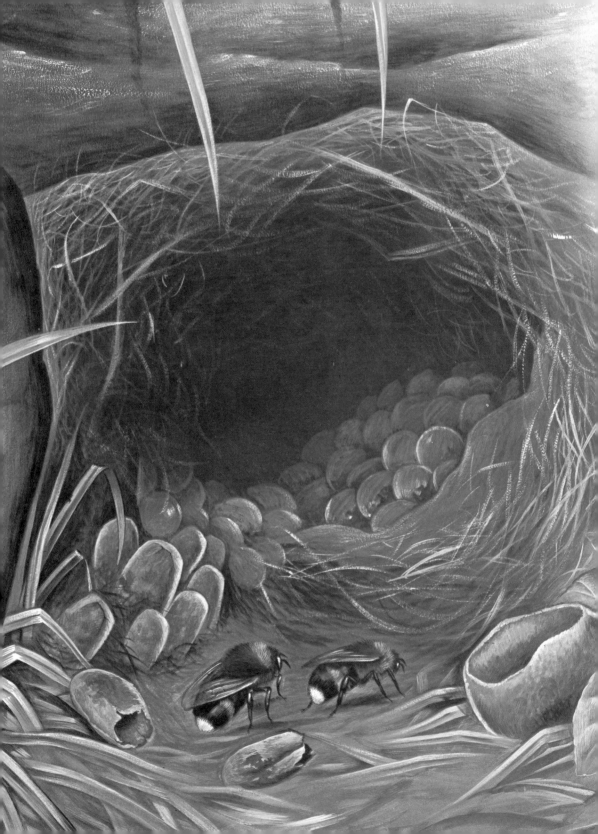

The queen carefully removed the cell from around the cocoons, and used the wax to help make new cells, ready for more eggs.

After all this work, the queen was very tired. But she would soon have help in the nest. Inside the cocoons, the little white grubs were slowly turning into bees. And, after about two weeks, the first brood struggled out of the silky cocoons. With wet wings drooping over their bodies, they were almost helpless.

The queen had to find more and more food for the young bees. All was well when the sun was shining. But for two days it did not stop raining and the queen could not go out. So she had to rely on the nectar stored in the honey-pot.

The wings of the young bees soon dried and they grew stronger and stronger. Now they could start work. The bees were all female workers. They had to help their mother feed and tend the grubs that were now growing up in the other cells. As fast as new cells were made, the queen filled them with eggs. Some of the workers stayed in the nest to feed the grubs. Others went out to collect more pollen and nectar. Some of the empty cocoons were used as honey-pots. When the workers came in from the meadow, carrying syrupy nectar and 'baskets' of powdery pollen, they filled the honey-pots.

Every day there were more and more grubs to feed in the cells. And each time a batch of cocoons burst open, there were eight, ten or even fourteen new bees. All of them were workers and the whole nest buzzed with the sound of their busyness.

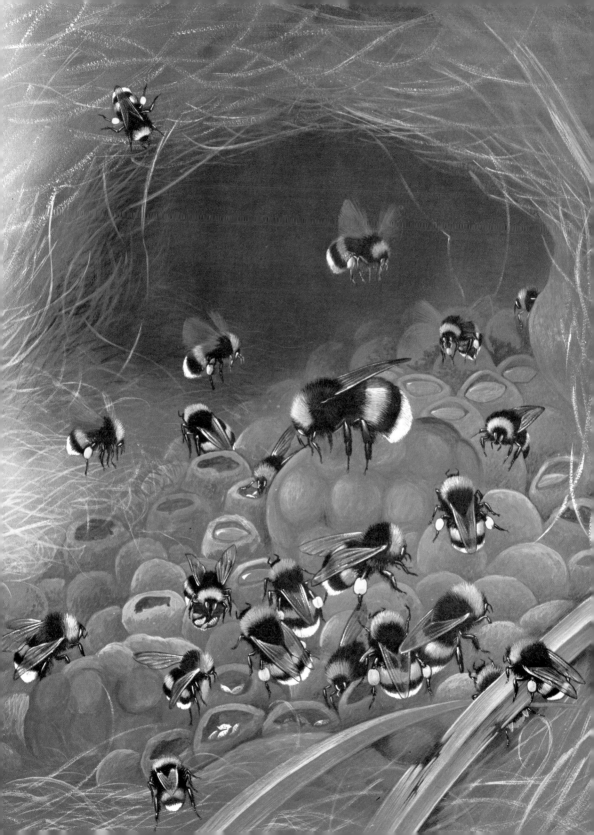

After a few months, the nest was so crowded with bees that it was almost impossible to count them. There were more than a hundred in the tiny space that was once a field mouse's nest. The workers had to keep adding new walls of dry grass to the front of the nest to make more room.

Outside, the fields and woods were full of flowers. In the meadow at the farm there was clover. In the hedgerows there was bindweed and deadnettle. And tall foxgloves grew along the edge of the wood.

But with so much food to gather, the workers still had to fly farther and farther each day to find new flowers. Sometimes they flew so far from the nest that they could not reach home by nightfall, and had to find a hiding place until morning. One worker even spent the night curled up in a foxglove flower. She was very weary when the dawn came, and her fur was wet with dew.

As this last bee was returning to the nest
after her night in the open, she saw the other
workers leaving to find flowers. They were fresh
and fit after a night in the nest. As they buzzed
out of the entrance, they flew straight into a young
badger. The badger should really have been back in
bed by this time, but it could smell the honey in the
nest and was trying to find it. Its claws were just
reaching for the grass around the door of the nest
when the bees inside felt its hot breath.

The bees used the only weapon they had to attack the badger. Crowding around, they stung it on the nose again and again. Instead of a tasty meal of bumblebees and honey, the badger fled with a sore and swollen nose.

If the badger's mother had attacked the nest, the result would have been different. Her tough nose could bear a few stings.

Although the nest was well hidden, the bees had to make sure that no other enemies attacked them. One of their enemies was very sly. It was a cuckoo bee. Cuckoos are birds that lay their eggs in other birds' nests. The cuckoo bee does the same thing in a bumblebee's nest. Once inside the nest, it hides until it smells like all the other bees and none of them notices it. Then it kills the queen and lays its own eggs in her cells. When the eggs hatch the bumblebee workers feed the grubs without knowing that they are tending their enemy's young.

One day a cuckoo bee did creep up on the nest. The workers were too busy to see it and it was right inside before they realized what had happened. A furious buzzing sounded in the nest. The workers left their tasks and swarmed towards the unwelcome visitor. The cuckoo bee lashed out with its sting and the first workers fell back, dead. But soon more bees arrived, all trying to sting the invader at once. The cuckoo bee did not give up. It pulled up its legs and its strong body was like armour against the workers' stings.

But the enraged workers fought on. In the end the stings of the bigger bees pierced the armoured body and the cuckoo bee lay dead. Its young would never be born and the bumblebees were safe.

All the workers in the nest were females. Towards the end of the summer, the queen laid fewer eggs. The last batches of eggs and grubs had so many workers to look after them and feed them that they grew very big indeed. When they broke out of their cocoons, they would be queen bees like their mother.

At the same time, too, the first male bees wriggled from their cocoons. Male bees are called drones. The drones were very lazy. They did no work at all. The new young queens did not do very much either.

But there was not much work to do now, anyway. The summer days were growing shorter and the flowers were beginning to disappear. One by one the workers grew too tired to go out and get food. As the flowers died, they died, too.

The queen was old and weary now. In one summer she had reared more than a hundred workers and twelve fine young queen bees. Her work was done. One evening she left the nest, settled drowsily on a meadow saffron and, as the sun faded, she fell into a deep sleep and died.

Within a few days, almost all the workers were dead. Only the young queens and drones were strong and healthy. They also had had to leave the nest. The drones left first, on their first trip into the air.

They did not go far from the nest because they wanted to mate with the young queens. The queens, too, felt the need to find a mate. So they flew from the nest high into the air.

As the queens flew, the drones followed them. Some were caught by drones from their own nest; others by drones from another nest that had been built near the farmhouse. One young queen flew high over the wood. She was followed closely by one of the farmhouse drones. As she grew tired, he clutched her in the air and they mated. A moment later the drone fell from the sky. He was dead.

Like all the other drones, he had flown only once. But in that flight he had made it possible for a whole new nest of bees to be born next summer.

Once she had mated, the queen flew on. In spring she would have to build a nest for her own eggs, as her mother had done. There would be no food for the new queen in the winter and the weather would be cruel and cold. She must quickly find a place to shelter.

The new queen spent some time feeding on the last of the summer flowers, and her body grew fat. As the autumn leaves fell, they made a brown carpet on the woodland floor. The queen bee crawled under some leaves at the foot of a tree and slowly went to sleep.

It would be more than six months before she woke. Rain, snow and hail would drench the wood, but she would be warm and safe.

More About Bumblebees

Where to see Bumblebees

Bumblebees are found all over the world, and there are many different kinds. Each kind has its own pattern of stripes and colours. Some are big, like the one in the story. Others are smaller. During the summer you can see worker bees almost anywhere, so long as there are flowers nearby. But you will probably only see queen bees early in the summer before their nests grow too big.

Food from Flowers

If there were no flowers, there would be no bumblebees. For bumblebees eat only nectar and pollen. They have good eyes and can find brightly coloured flowers very easily. When a bumblebee settles on a flower, it sucks up nectar with its tongue. The tongue is a hollow tube. It is so long that the bumblebee has to fold it under its head when it is not feeding.

The bumblebee does not use up all the nectar that it sucks up. It stores some inside its body and brings it back for the younger bees to eat. The nectar is changed into honey and stored in 'honey-pots' in the nest.

Baskets of Pollen

As well as nectar, bumblebees collect and eat pollen. If you look closely at a bumblebee's back legs, you will often see balls of yellow pollen clinging to them. The pollen is stuck firmly on to rows of strong, stiff hairs that grow down each side of the legs. The hairs make a kind of basket. As the bee feeds, pollen is brushed off the flower on to its furry body. The bee then neatly combs the pollen off its back on to its legs. When it reaches home, the bee sweeps the pollen from the baskets into cells, so that there is always a good store. The bumblebee may gather as much as half its weight in pollen in one trip.

As a bee lands on a flower, it may brush on to it some of the pollen gathered from the one before. This is good for the flower, because the flower needs the pollen from another flower to make its seeds. Without bees and other insects that carry pollen some flowers would never have any seeds. So the flowers need the bees as much as the bees need the flowers.

Wax Works

The queen bee and the workers make cells for the nest with wax. Some of the pollen the bees swallow turns into wax inside their bodies. When the bee squeezes certain muscles, the wax oozes out from between 'plates' of tough skin underneath the body. The bee moulds this wax with its two jaws before shaping it into cells.

worker

queen

drone

The three kinds of bumblebee

Buzz Buzz Buzz

You can often hear a bumblebee long before you catch sight of it. All the time they are flying about their wings make a buzzing noise, like the hum of a tiny aeroplane. Bumblebees are often called humble bees because of this.

Sting in the Tail

Everyone knows that bees sting. But there is no need to be too scared of them. Bumblebees are gentle creatures. They only use their stings if they are attacked or annoyed. The sting is a tiny 'tube' in the bee's tail. The bee pierces its enemy's skin with the sharp point and then squirts poison through it. The poison is strong enough to kill some animals.

Honeybees have stings with little points called barbs down the sides. When they use their sting, it sometimes gets caught in their victim's flesh and cannot be pulled out again. This means that the bee has to leave its sting behind when it flies off. So it can sting only once. Bumblebee stings have no barbs so they can sting again and again.

Enemies Big and Small

Despite their stings, bumblebees have many enemies. The bee-eater is a bird that eats them. It is very clever at catching them in its beak and not being stung. Bigger animals such as mice, shrews, skunks and badgers also like to eat bees. But it is smaller animals that do most harm to bumblebees. Like the cuckoo bee, the wax moth invades bumblebee nests. When the caterpillars hatch, they tunnel through the nest, breaking up the cells and eating the wax, so that many eggs and grubs die. The robber fly is another dangerous enemy. It catches bumblebees in mid air and sucks their blood with its sharp beak.

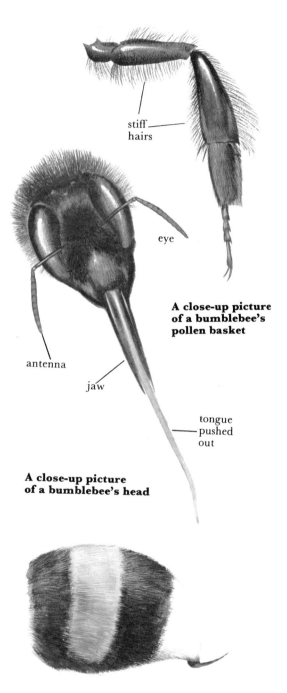

stiff hairs

eye

A close-up picture of a bumblebee's pollen basket

antenna

jaw

tongue pushed out

A close-up picture of a bumblebee's head

A bumblebee's sting